JOAN THE SAINT

by

STANISLAS FUMET

Translated by

F. J. SHEED

NEW YORK
SHEED AND WARD
1937

NIHIL OBSTAT: REGINALDUS PHILLIPS, S.TH.L.

CENSOR DEPUTATUS

IMPRIMATUR: L. CAN. EVANS,

VIC. GEN.

WESTMONASTERII, DII 17A MARTII 1937

Joan of Arc assisting at the Coronation of Charles VII in
Rheims Cathedral

From the painting by   Ingres, in the Louvre, Paris

JOAN THE SAINT

JOAN THE SAINT

I

WHEN there is nowhere left to turn, when the best laid schemes of princes have a decidedly battered look, when hope falls broken before an obstacle too towering, when all seems lost and surrender the only wisdom, when, in short, man is totally helpless – then is the favourable moment for the angels of God.

There was a deep-lying distress, something altogether pitiful, in the kingdom of France; discouragement, deadness, a kind of death. And that very deadness, it would seem, roused to action another kind of life: for it drew God's attention and moved God's heart. There was no outward activity, nothing that you would notice. But there was a coming-and-going of angels – those angels in particular whose business it is to weave the thread of mercy between Heaven and earth.

The kingdom of France, consecrated by St. Louis, saw itself growing daily less. Charles VI was dead. The Dauphin, who presumably had some shred of ambition to preserve the realm which a dwindling few – the more generous perhaps – regarded as his, withdrew steadily southward.

In 1429 the English took Orleans. The Dauphin withdrew to Chinon, and meditated leaving France to agonize without him; he planned a flight into Spain.

No one could forget the crime of Isabella, his mother. In alliance with the Duke of Burgundy she persuaded Charles VI – Charles the Mad, alternatively known as Charles the Beloved – to sign the Treaty of Troyes, handing over the country to the English. But even that did not suffice her. She planted a mortal ailment in the heart of Charles, her son, giving him to understand that he was not of the blood royal, not the king's son. The young man, by way of consolation for the towns he was losing, played with dissipation:

at night, in his own room, the laughter died from his face, as he took his head in his hands and conjured God to show him truly if he were the rightful heir to the crown of France.

England grew bigger and bigger, swelled beyond her borders in proportion as France grew smaller, fading towards nothingness like the identity of her poor prince. Faithless Burgundy opened all her roads, and down them the English thronged, to crush with heavy measured tread the humiliated land of France. For England it was a gigantic victory, breath-taking, intoxicating; it ended the Hundred Years War, and filled to overflowing the cup of her desires.

Was there any heart in which the King of Heaven might come to dwell? Was there not – in the Marches of Lorraine, perhaps – a child's heart so virginal that it might contain something of His Will, some spark from His Omnipotence? What God wanted, what His work needed then as ever, was a virgin whose virginity should be not only a fact but *the* fact, not simply a condition of her being, but the very purpose of her being; one who should be not merely a maid but *the* maid – La Pucelle.

God loves to show His glory in a subject that has nothing of its own. He loves that His own power should be all in all in the creature. Where weakness is pitiful He establishes His own strength. Where humility is total He builds an edifice of His own splendour. And like lightning the angels came forth from Him to re-make the Kingdom of France which Joan had already re-made in her own heart.

She was thirteen. She lived in Domremy and spun hemp and tended her father's cattle. All spoke her praises – from the parish priest to the beggars on the roads, including the parents she loved, Jacques d'Arc and his wife Isabelle, and all the neighbours and the village children, those she played with – Hauviette, her special friend, and the others. The only fault they could find with her was excessive devotion to God and a taste for pilgrimages. When the others played, it was her pleasure to make wreaths for Our Lady. She loved above all to go aside and 'Speak with God'. But she was a hard worker. It was her joy to be with the sick, and she showed great tenderness for the poor, the tenderness which always goes with, and never goes without, the love of God.

At Domremy she gave the poor her own bed. Later she was to declare that she had 'come to console the poor and the needy'. And Pasquerel, her chaplain, who was at all her battles and never left her from Orleans to Compiègne, has left us this luminous testimony: 'She was deeply devoted to God and Our Blessed Lady; went to Confession almost every day, and to Communion frequently. In Confession she wept. When she was in a place where there was a convent of Mendicants, she told me to remind her of the day on which the children received Communion that she might receive it with them. . . .'

Joan was thirteen when St. Michael spoke to her the first time. But she did not know for certain whose voice it was; she did not realize that it came from an angel till the third time that she heard it. On the first occasion she was much afraid. It was noon of a summer's day; she was in her father's garden; she suddenly heard the voice calling upon her 'to bear herself aright'. That for her was the whole matter: to make straight towards the goal – *straight*. At her trial in Rouen she stated that it was not the day after a fast day. . . . 'I heard this voice to my right, towards the church; I rarely hear it without seeing a light at the same time.'

Often after that, either alone or 'surrounded by the angels of Heaven', St. Michael spoke to her and she realized that he bore a message from God. One day he commanded her: 'Go to France!'

When it was not St. Michael who visited Joan, it was his and her two friends, St. Catherine and St. Margaret. They also came to her as voices, but they showed themselves as faces and Joan touched

12

their bodies. She even kissed them, and this bore heavily against her with her judges.

Near Domremy there was a great beech called the Fairy Tree, straight and beautiful 'as a lily'. On Laetare Sunday it was the custom for the children to sing in its shade and circle it in their dances, after which they would eat, and go off to slake their thirst at the Fontaine des Groseillers. Joan went there like the others, but she preferred to sing and weave garlands rather than dance. The sinister crew of clerics and lawyers in Rouen and Paris based the whole infamous process upon the insinuation that Joan had vowed herself to the devil under the Fairy Tree, and had uttered incantations at the fountain. It is true that the saints spoke to her at the fountain, but she kept no special memory of what they told her there more than elsewhere.

She hesitated long. She was a prudent, sensible girl, not given to easy credulity. The voices had to return to the charge; God had to reveal Himself very clearly, very definitely before the child would embrace the idea of leaving her father's house. Her father in fact had a dream about it; he saw her going off with soldiers. Fortunately it was only a dream: he would rather have drowned her in the Meuse out of hand.

At this time there was a saying current: 'A girl will come from the Bois Chesnu and will ride on the backs of archers. France, lost by a woman, will be saved by a maiden from the Marches of Lorraine.'

Behind Domremy there was a wood which was, in fact, called the Bois Chesnu. All this helped to convince Joan. From thirteen to eighteen she firmly withstood her voices; at last she could withstand them no longer. The Maid of Lorraine arose and turned her eyes towards Orleans, which was in the possession of the English. In this decision there is a hint of Our Lady repairing the ill work of Eve. Thus Joan the Maid went to the Seigneur Robert de Baudricourt, at Vaucouleurs. She hoped to get from him equipment and men to pay a surprise visit to the melancholy Dauphin who was dreaming

14

of Spain; for the Maid wished to make him King.
In the name of God he must be King of France –
he, so cruelly disinherited by his mother of all he
possessed in mind and soul and body. He deserved
God's aid because his cause was lost – lamentably
lost.

Now that Joan of Arc is canonized, the bare fact illumines all her work from within. One word is the key to her history – the word GO!

From the age of thirteen it beat upon her ear like a trumpet note, and more than human words sounded with it: 'Go, child of God, child of the Church, child of great heart!' She could withhold obedience no longer.

At Vaucouleurs she approached Robert, who held the town for the Dauphin. He laughed at the audacious, red-clad child who talked of her Lord – *her* Lord – and said to Robert that 'he must tell the Dauphin to hold himself firm, not to abandon the war, that the Lord would come to his aid before the middle of the following Lent; that the realm of France did not belong to *him*, the Dauphin, but to her Lord; that her Lord wished the Dauphin to be king and to hold the realm in stewardship, that she would make him king despite his enemies, and would bring him to his coronation'.

'But who and what is this "Lord" you speak of?' asked Robert.

'The King of Heaven,' she answered.

Robert de Baudricourt advised her uncle to whip her and send her back home to her father. But she did not lose heart; she was merely impatient to see the king:

'The time seemed long to her as to a woman with child,' and she said that she would go to Chinon, even if she had 'to wear her legs down to the knees'. But several knights believed in her; they persuaded her to doff her woman's clothing and got her a man's costume with full military equipment, and gave her a horse. Then they escorted her – Bertrand de Poulengey, and his servant, Jean de Metz; and Jean de Honecourt and his servant, Colet de Vienne and Richard l'Archer – travelling mainly by night for fear of the English and the Burgundians who controlled the roads.

At Chinon, where the Dauphin was, they made quiet entry at the end of the eleventh day.

It is at this point that the supernatural character of Joan's mission begins to appear in all its profundity – and it is precisely here that it is usually overlooked by her biographers. The testimonies are unanimous about her simplicity:

'A very simple girl, except in the matter of war, wherein she excelled,' said the soldiers. But the same soldiers took her for a miracle; it was sufficient to fight under her banner, or to lie beside her at night, to have the certitude that she was a saint. Joan's sanctity really is something like Heaven on the human level. She lived in all innocence in the spiritual world with Michael and his legions of angels, with St. Margaret and St. Catherine; and at the same time her feet were kept firmly on the ground by a nature, positive, objective, cheerful – above all by that woman's weakness which made her shrink a little at the approach of suffering — another's or her own.

When this humble, audacious girl presented herself before Charles VII, recognized him although
he was disguised among his courtiers, went straight
to him as it was her habit to go, Joan of Arc was
more than a human being: the whole Court of
Heaven went with her. Her message was wholly
bound up with that mysterious kingship which she
came to offer the Dauphin in supernatural terms.
Joan offered Heaven to France, bleeding from its
wounds; to the broken land of Charlemagne and
St. Louis she offered the ineffable arms of the God
of Hosts. She told her judges later, in tones of
triumph and of ecstasy, that it was not herself – the
Maid – but an angel who had given her King that
miraculous, mysterious crown, the mere thought of
which, for all their earthly incredulity, was so dis-
turbing to them as servants of victorious England.

The angels of Paradise thronged about the one
angel who 'came from on high, entered through
the door of the room, made reverence to the king,
bowing before him'. As for the crown she spoke

of, it was the sign of which there was question throughout the trial.

'Where is this sign of yours?'

'My sign is in the King's Treasury.'

The saints exist only to sanctify the earth. We must elevate ourselves to their place, and not imagine them abased to ours, if we are to understand their words and actions aright. Joan was 'a child of God'. This holy, visionary peasant girl walked in Heaven while she walked on earth. It was not the son of Isabella that she adored, and in whom she saw the best of Christians; it was not the ungrateful boy whom she saluted with her hood; it was He to whom that unseen crown was dedicated. In that poor wreck of a king she honoured the bearer of God's mandate in France.

For her, the scene of her meeting with the Dauphin was laid in Heaven. Herein Joan revealed the solution of the prime political problem, and there is no other. It was the solution given her by God through St. Michael and St. Catherine and

St. Margaret; the simple truth that the earth belongs to no man, but only to the King of Heaven. It is entrusted in stewardship to the hands of men who must hold it for the Creator. That is why Joan, the moment she was in the Dauphin's room – along with the Duc d'Alençon, who reports the event, and the Sire de la Trémouille – begged the king of France that 'he should make gift of his realm to the King of Heaven'.

Thus the supernatural and the natural can be rightly interwoven in the ordering of the realm, provided always that there is no prevarication on the part of the vassal. Hold this fact clear: since Israel there has been no political truth so certain.

Joan inaugurated the doctrine of Christ the King, the doctrine whereby human sovereignty is absorbed in the sovereignty of God. Small matter that it has been ill understood; small matter that Charles VII made haste to betray her. In herself she demonstrated what this polity could mean by her work in that year, by the totally unforeseeable turn she gave to the war; above all by her suffering and death which will stand for ever as an image of the suffering and death of Our Lord.

She revealed to the Dauphin that he was the rightful heir, for she had learnt in a vision all that secret anxiety which he kept so jealously within himself; and she had told him that she had been sent to communicate to him that his anxiety was unfounded. At that word he was overcome with emotion, and upon the instant he believed in Joan.

After being examined and interrogated at Poitiers and declared truthful, Joan the Maid raised the siege of Orleans to the amazement of the boldest captains of the realm, the Bastard of Orleans, the Duc d'Alençon and the Sire de Gaucourt. The English had the strength and the numbers; they had the arms, especially those superb crossbows that the French lacked; they were organized, accustomed to victory, properly certain of victory to come.

'Do not fear their numbers,' said the girl, from the back of her white steed; 'don't hesitate to give

the assault; God will guide your enterprise. . . .'
Then, with no waste of time, behind the banner of
the Maid they attacked Jargeau, Meung-sur-Loir,
Beaugency and Patay, which fell one by one. The
whole of her strategic genius which was incredible,
she obtained only from her 'Counsel'. Before
Orleans she said to Dunois:

'Are you the Bastard of Orleans?'

'Yes; and I am very glad of your arrival!'

'Is it you who said that I should come from this
side, and not go directly to the side where Talbot
and the English are?'

'Yes; and wiser men than I are of the same
opinion. . . .'

'In the Name of God,' she said then, 'the counsel
of my Lord is wiser and surer than yours!'

She never took action – whether in the making
of war or in the answering of her judges – without
having direction from above. Of her Counsel,
we know this on the testimony of Jean d'Aulon,
her steward:

'Her counsellors were three, of whom one was always with her, the second came and went often and visited her, and the third was the One with whom the other two deliberated.'

She lived prayer more than she actually prayed, her mind and will were wholly and utterly and heroically given to God. At Orleans men and women and children ran after her to touch her garments. In their eyes she was not a girl but an angel of God.

Her warfare was an active peace. Herein we see the supernatural quality of her vocation; in the incredible work she accomplished in a year, we see the hand of the Lord of the Heavenly Hosts who had cried before rebellious Lucifer: 'May God crush you!'

She who was a soldier only through obedience worked in exactly the same fashion. She had no warlike will, her will indeed was no longer her own, because she had chosen the Will of God. The spirits of the blessed had persuaded her to exchange her will for God's at Domremy. What she found utterly astonishing was that men should resist God. She simply let herself be handled by Him as a lance is handled. At need she has the air of giving orders; but she is merely transmitting orders. Did she reflect? Very little: she obeyed her Voices and the luminous directions she received. She raised her standard and that was a gesture: she was Christian confidence incarnate.

Like those friends of God who were her friends, Joan had a sword. It was a strange sword which had been discovered behind an altar in the church of St. Catherine at Ferbois following one of her visions. She was herself the sword in God's hand, and why should she unsheath her human sword, miraculous though it might be? She rode with a banner in her hand 'in order not to use her sword', she explained, 'not to kill anyone'. Her weapon upraised was her banner, the symbol of glory, a background of sky with the image of Jesus Christ

25

she had had painted on it, holding the world in His right hand, an angel on either side of Him.

At sight of her banner the English were seized with panic. It had been impossible to dislodge them from France. Dunois, d'Alençon, La Hire, Xaintrailles, had put all their heart, all their science, all their energy into dislodging them, and the English stood like a stone wall – immovable: they even advanced a little, to the further reduction of the realm of France. But when the Maid appeared with the white banner in her hand, and that victim-clearness in the youngness of her face, English confidence was at an end; victory was no longer certain! It seemed that there was a 'charm' in the French camp. They swore against her, spat at her name, blasphemed Joan and her purity, hurled insults at her from behind their lines so that the tears came to her eyes. But they trembled, and did not know what they feared, and abandoned their most assured positions. Her troops followed her in a kind of trance.

26

Her deepest sorrow was to see the blood of others flow – whether friends or enemies. When the Tower of Orleans was taken Joan was wounded as she had foretold the previous evening, by an arrow which 'penetrated half a foot between her neck and her shoulder': she did not cease to fight until her army held the place, but the day after the great battle, when the English were drawn up to retire, she forbade her men 'to attack or to demand anything of them since she wished that they should be allowed to go unpursued, which they did'.

From that moment, adds Dunois, 'the town was delivered'. This same Bastard of Orleans tells us how Joan had had help from God to win the battle; sorely wounded, she refused all attention for herself. 'The assault lasted without interruption from the morning until eight o'clock in the evening.' The situation seemed desperate. Dunois wished to abandon the place, but the Maid came to him and urged him to be patient.

'Whereupon she mounted her horse, withdrew

to a vineyard, and alone, far from the others, she remained in prayer for a quarter of an hour; then returned, and seizing her banner in both hands, she stood on the edge of the trench. A sudden panic seized the English. . . . It was the angel of God beneath the armour of the Maid that terrified them.'

At Beaugency, La Hire commanded a vanguard. Joan was upset at this, for she loathed the slaughters that he loved to make. In this case he caused a terrible massacre of the English. Joan was filled with pity. A Frenchman, whose task it was to lead the prisoners away, had just half murdered one of them. The Maid got down from her horse and went to the Englishman, 'got him to confess his sins, holding his head the while and consoling him as best she might'.

It is necessary to grasp the orientation to peace of Joan's vocation. What she truly aimed at, in the victorious campaign she waged, was the extermination of war. For in it the destiny of the kingdom

28

was in the hands of God, and usurped territory was given back, foot by foot, into the rightful hands, like a beach as the tide recedes. She ordered the movement of her armies, but it was from Heaven that the orders came. But if they came from God she translated them pretty freely, in a way to suit her own mind and heart and mouth. She is full of magnificent phrases. She wrote to the English: 'You men of England who have no right in this realm, the King of Heaven orders you, through me, Joan the Maid, to leave your towers and return to your own country: if not I shall make such an uproar that the memory thereof will last for ever. . . .'

She was quick of tongue, especially quick of retort, agile in body, prompt and free of soul, but she lived spiritually between Heaven and earth. In her eyes France was a screen and the Will of God played upon it. For her and by her there was a sacred action to be carried out in the realm of France, an action which was the temporal showing of a problem of eternal justice. Obviously she did not realize the implications of all her ideas. She lived by faith rather than by philosophy. But, seeing herself as a mere instrument, a humble but powerful soldier, strongly attached to the banner of God's peace, she accomplished the work of the Divine King which makes its own luminous path through our darkness. She lived her mysticism in a life of war, because God so willed. All that lived so intensely in her soul shaped itself to an exterior realization beyond parallel. St. Thérèse of Lisieux made a very searching comment on St. Joan's mission when she said that the goal of everyone of us is to drive the invader from all the territory he occupies in our souls, and to bring back the true King to be anointed in them.

The supreme question was the anointing of the king, and his coronation at Reims. For the anointing meant to Joan, not the legalization of his earthly titles, but the divinization of his kingship. The first thing the king must offer to God was the realm,

which henceforth he must simply rule in stewardship. Christ is the sole King; but the king of
France, having sworn submission and fealty, is His
lieutenant. When Charles VII had undertaken this
total surrender into God's hands of the kingdom
that he received only as God's representative, Joan
used one splendid phrase: 'Behold you,' she said,
'the poorest knight in your kingdom!'

The ceremonial anointing, at which Joan stood a
few paces from the king, standard in hand, was the
solemn confirmation of what she had promised
Charles: 'The King of Heaven assures you through
me that you will be anointed and crowned at
Reims, and that you will be the lieutenant of the
King of Heaven, who is King of France.'

The good town of Reims, which was still in the
hands of the English, but which Joan had begged
by letter to surrender as she had begged Chalons
and Troyes, opened its gates at her request, and the
citizens of Reims went out in procession to welcome
King Charles VII. It is the plain truth that the

coronation which took place in the Cathedral, with the vessel of holy oil, amid a fanfare of trumpets, was an alliance between France and Heaven brought about by the sanctity of Joan of Arc.

But, alas, neither Charles VII nor any other king could or would fulfil the conditions of the alliance. Only sanctity holds to its word. Yet Joan, who lived in the light of angels and showed forth as she might the splendour of God's plan, Joan who could, at Lagny, bring back to life a child three days dead simply that it might be baptized, Joan never for one moment doubted that Charles VII would be faithful to an alliance so advantageous. She loved her king as the temporal figure of the Kingdom of Christ. And he? The day after his coronation his one thought was to take a rest from the glory that had come upon him too rapidly. The poor wretch had had enough. Joan's head was in the heavens, and the air was more than he could breathe.

She saw that the English had to be completely

driven out of France: Charles VII did not see it. The lieutenant of God preferred to listen to Regnault de Chartres and La Trémouille – bad counsellors, jealous of the girl's influence. Paris was demoralized, and would have yielded. Instead of marching upon it, Charles dreamed of a truce. He established himself at Compiègne and let Joan go off alone to plant her banner under the walls of Paris. He made a half-hearted pretence of going to join her, stopped at Senlis, sent the Duc d'Alençon to Joan, recalled him, and finally forced Joan to retire to St. Denis. Joan was terrified and poured forth her lamentations, for they were disobeying her voices. There remained but one thing for her to do – to make an attack by the other bank of the Seine which she hoped to gain with the aid of a bridge built by the Duc d'Alençon.

In the morning, though wounded in the thigh by an arrow, she got ready to renew the attack with all her men. But during the night the bridge had been demolished by order of Charles VII.

God's too human lieutenant had deliberately betrayed the saint. From the moment when the king, with all that his anointing implied, betrayed Joan's divine mission, there was an unsureness in all her operations. She was no longer free. Her will had been God's Will, but now a third will, mediocre and commonplace, was bringing disorder into her programme which was the angels' programme. Charles VII went off again towards the Loire. We know now that he had entered into a secret treaty with the Burgundians. To make Joan give up the attack on Paris – Paris which was soon to make her its own – he had her recalled from St. Denis. From September 13, 1429, Joan and the Duc d'Alençon followed the king; then she and d'Alençon separated. Joan remained at Bourges, took Saint-Pierre-Le Moustier in November, and laid unsuccessful siege – in the silence of her voices – to La Charité-sur-Loire. She remained several months with the king and queen. Then, weary of that, and urged on by her overmastering passion to clear the English out of France, she left the Château de Sully without taking leave of the king, and, together with d'Alençon, Pasquerel and their people, set out for Paris. She defeated the Burgundians and the English at Lagny; at Melun on Easter Sunday her voices told her that she would be seized, that it must be so, and that she must accept it with good grace.

At last, on May 23, 1430, fifteen months after her departure from Domremy, twelve months after the deliverance of Orleans, she betook herself for the fourth time to Compiègne at 'the secret hour of the morning' with a force of four hundred or five hundred men, with the idea of saving this town to which the English and Burgundians had already laid siege. There Joan fell into an ambush, was hurled off her horse by five or six archers who forced her to surrender to them. She was handed over to Jean de Luxembourg, a vassal of the Duke of Burgundy. From that fatal hour she became the prey of the enemies of God, who held her in torment a whole year 'in the name of the Devil', the charming phrase which burst one day from the lips of the usually more cautious Cauchon. Her heart was wrung, her soul filled with desolation. At night she had to struggle against the English soldiers who strove to violate her. All the evil forces of baptized man false to his baptism rose together against the fragile impregnable citadel personified by the child of God, the incorruptible Maid who dressed like a boy and who was almost an angel.

III

How dare we reproach Israel of old for having condemned its Messias to death, since we Christians, when a faintly similar case appeared in our history, were not slow to do likewise? It is altogether in conformity with human nature, damaged by sin, to hate the Just and the man sent by God. Joan's trial reproduces so mysteriously the trial of God by the Sanhedrin that it is not to be recalled without a quickening of shame. For the scandalous affair of Joan, the Sanhedrin was present in force. Abbots of monasteries and theologians of repute came to join with the secular clergy of the diocese. The Bishop of Beauvais, Maître Pierre Cauchon, had paid the Duke of Burgundy a great price – ten thousand *livres* – in order to have God's hostage in his hands. The sum is unbelievable for that time. It was a king's ransom. But England would have paid a world for her if so much had been necessary.

When Joan learnt that the Burgundians meant to sell her to the English, she threw herself from the top of the tower of Beaurevoir – not to kill herself, as her enemies suggested, but as a last hope of escaping the vengeance of the English and saving her friends in Compiègne. This act of temerity – so her voices affirmed – was forgiven her. When the tribunal asked her if she had done penance for this abominable action, she replied that the pain she had had of the fall was assuredly penance enough.

The 'Reverend Father in Christ and Lord', Pierre Cauchon, claimed the right to judge the Maid in Rouen, pushing his claim against the University of Paris which hated Joan no less profoundly than he. Three French authorities – the University, the Inquisition, and Bishop Cauchon – strove together for the glory of condemning the innocent girl whose strong humility, one presumes, had cast a spell upon God, since she was accused of nothing less than sorcery and magic when she had indeed worked miracles. The Inquisition would have been the best qualified for the task, for it was at that time the most impartial of tribunals. But the Duke of Bedford, who governed England as Regent for the child king, Henry VI, would take no chances of delivering Joan to any tribunal that was not certain to find her guilty. The Bishop of Beauvais was Bedford's dependent. The town of Beauvais had just become French once more, and Cauchon did not dream of going back to it, though it was his own diocese. But by great good fortune Rouen was, for the moment, without an archbishop. It was easy for England's creature to have himself given a more or less regular jurisdiction over the territory and diocese of the town. Further, Bedford promised Cauchon to have him made Archbishop of Rouen. A correspondence dripping with unction and supreme hypocrisy was entered into between the University of Paris and Maître Cauchon. Cauchon, to prevent any possible chance of justice for his prisoner, had her incarcerated, not in the ecclesiastical prison as the law required when an accusation bore on a matter of faith, but in a fortress in the hands of the English. Then he set on foot a trial of which the echoes are sounding still. Every detail of it has come down to us.

We find gathered together the Pharisees and Scribes – only a little more frightful than their prototypes of Jerusalem because they signed themselves with the divine Name of Jesus and offered up Mass daily in all peace of conscience. There were the English soldiery – the Romans of this story; there was the little king, Henry VI, now aged nine, brought over specially to see the famous prisoner. He lived in the same castle as she. There was a populace of English and Burgundians, anxiously waiting for the death sentence. Joan even had her Barabbas, for there was a custom at Rouen, on the Feast of the Ascension, to set free a prisoner. The choice fell on a bandit whose only crime was robbery.

The mind revolts from dwelling on the men who

composed the tribunal: there was, for instance, the Canon Jean d'Estivet, his mouth full of filthy insults which he came to pour out by Joan's bedside when she was ill. Or think for a moment of the priest Loyseleur, who won Joan's friendship so that he might get her to make her confession to him aloud, his idea being to have clerks hidden behind the curtain to take it all down. The plan failed, because this was lower than those decent men were prepared to go.

In 1450, at the time of her rehabilitation, all those who still lived confessed that they had acted only for fear of the bishop and the English. Certain it is that all who were suspected of the least sympathy for Joan were threatened with being flung into the Seine. But of all this fester of iniquity nothing appeared on the surface, and the trial proceeded on its stately way in unimpeachable form.

One of the charges that recurs most insistently had to do with the clothes she wore. Even in prison she had chosen not to change her soldier's garb. Once when she was in France curious women asked her why she chose to dress as a man, and she answered that it was more convenient to make war clad thus; and, besides that, dressed like a man she would be less likely to arouse lust of the flesh in the soldiers, and would 'the better preserve her virginity in thought and deed'. But at the same time there were more mystical elements in her choice, which she would not reveal to her judges, saying only that it was Our Lord's will and not her own that she should dress as a man.

'As far as clothes are concerned, it is a small matter – less than nothing. . . . I have taken this dress, not on the advice of any man; I have neither taken this dress nor done anything save by command of Our Lord and the angels.'

Her soldier's dress, for all that, irritated them beyond everything. They forbade her to come to Mass, and this was her most grievous sorrow. Why, then, when they assured her that if she gave up her soldier's clothing they would let her hear Mass, did she give no direct reply? The truth was that she saw clearly into the deceit of their minds. 'Do you think to take me by this means and draw me to you?' she answered them. If she refused to give a direct reply, it was because their questions, as she read in their souls, were not sincere. She listened, not to the sound of words, but to the movement of the heart; the heart was her kingdom. Not for her to answer a lie with a truth it did not deserve. With hard scorn she met the weakness of their pride and impurity.

That there was a mystical reason for dressing as a man we cannot doubt. Her voices never allowed her to yield on the point. 'In all I refer to Our Lord.' Another phrase, splendid as the light of Paradise, she uttered upon the matter of her mysterious choice of dress: 'I have never done anything save by the order of God.' It was Our Lord who ordered her to dress in this wise, with her hair clipped short above her ears, and the soldier's dress

43

made for war and for the guarding of her chastity. There was something of the angel in her mission, and something of the angel in her appearance. The men who followed her standard declared that she had always seemed to them stronger than nature. It astonished them to see the length of time she could stay in the saddle, to see her living on a crust of bread and drinking almost nothing. Wounded, she continued to head the assault. Joan had so much of the angel in her that she could, without peril, dress like the soldiers.

At the hour of her abjuration – the most sorrowful hour of her life – Joan agreed to change into woman's clothing. A few days later, after an Englishman had tried to violate her by night, she returned to her man's clothes which had been left of set purpose at her door; and in the morning they found her dressed as of old, in a very agony of affliction, her face bathed in tears. Whereupon they judged her relapsed.

Questioned as to her salvation she invariably showed admirable confidence. Her words ought to be remembered.

'Do you know whether you are in the grace of God?'

'If I am not, God will put me therein; and if I am, God will guard me therein. I should be the most miserable of creatures if I knew that I were not in God's grace. . . . But if I were in a state of sin, do you think that the voice would come to me?'

Another day: 'Do you hold yourself certain to be saved, and not to be damned in hell?'

'I believe firmly what my voices have told me – that I shall be saved; I believe it as firmly as if I were already in heaven.'

'After this revelation, do you believe that you can never again commit mortal sin?'

'I know nothing of that, and I leave all to Our Lord.'

'That is a reply of great weight?'

'Yes; and I hold it as a great treasure.'

On the afternoon of the same day, under further questioning, she completed her reply: 'Provided that I keep the promise I have made Our Lord to preserve the virginity of my body and my soul.'

Joan of Arc's virginity is a virtue which has not been sufficiently meditated. It was not only men but her voices who called her Joan the Maid. This we know from her own mouth. Of necessity she had to attach to this mystery of virginity a supernatural importance.

There is most obviously a point in which Joan resembles Our Lord. She had come to save her people, and she was delivered to an ignominious death by the Scribes and Pharisees of her people. This girl, who could neither read nor write, uttered words that could not have been invented, words that inevitably recalled the language of Our Lord: 'I am come from God: I have naught to do here. Let me be sent back to God whence I am come.'

There is an equally inevitable comparison with

Our Lady. It was not her virginity that counted, but the reflection of Mary's virginity in hers – that virginity which brought forth the salvation of the human race. Thus we come to see that it was from her virginity that Joan of Arc drew the strength which she had – the strength which she was. It was to her unbearable that any perverse thing should be said of her maidenhood. It was the supreme sacrilege, and a blasphemy that seemed to her to strike at the sanctity of Our Lady herself.

The Maid was troubled to the depths of her soul when her poor virtue was insulted. As she came into Chinon a man asked if that was not the Maid. Then he swore with a horrible blasphemy that if he had her a night, he would not give her back as he received her.

'In God's Name,' said Joan, 'you deny God and you are close to death!'

An hour after he was drowned.

To offer insults to her virginity was dangerous, as Clasdas found, who commanded the English in

Orleans. Joan had had one of her archers shoot an arrow with a letter to the English attached: from her camp she cried out:

'Read! It is something new!'

When the English had read the letter, which called upon them to surrender, they began to shout out: 'Here is news sent us by the harlot of the Armagnacs!'

Joan sobbed. Then she prayed for long. In the afternoon of the next day she was grievously wounded in the shoulder. She was afraid, and wept; yet she refused to be 'charmed' by magic. Her wound was dressed. She went to Confession in tears; then returned in all haste to the assault, crying: 'Clasdas! Clasdas! Surrender! Surrender to the King of Heaven! You called me harlot; I have great pity on your soul and your men's souls!' At that instant, so Pasquerel tells us, Clasdas fell, armed from head to foot, into the Loire where he was drowned.

Later on, at Rouen, when she was recovering

from illness, she was insulted in the same manner
by Jean d'Estivet; she burst into sobs, and her fever
returned. This same d'Estivet they found one day
dead in a ditch.

In the camp her chastity produced extraordinary
effects. The evidence of her soldiers, brought
together for her rehabilitation, leaves this in no
doubt. 'She was as pure as an angel,' declared
Bertrand de Poulengey, who was with her from
Vaucouleurs to Chinon. From the Duc d'Alençon
we learn how great was her loathing for the women
who followed the army. One day she pursued one,
sword in hand; 'her sword broke just at that
moment', and d'Alençon adds: 'Sometimes during
the war I lay by her in the straw, I and other
soldiers besides; I could see her when she was
putting on her armour, and could catch sight of
her breast, which was very beautiful, yet I never
felt evil desires for her.' All the evidence of her
companions agrees upon this, that it was impossible
to feel sinful desire for the Maid.

D 49

In the original text there is that most notable account told by Jean d'Aulon of the warlike feats of Joan. In it we read: 'For all that she was a girl, beautiful and shapely, and that on several occasions both in helping her to arm and otherwise he had seen her breast and many times her legs, quite naked, when he was dressing her wounds, and that he was oftentimes near her and was strong and young and vigorous; yet never for any sight or touch he had of the said Maid was his body moved to any carnal desire in her regard; nor likewise any other of her soldiers and esquires, as he who speaks has heard them say and tell many times.'

And there is this still more sublime deposition of Dunois, the Bastard of Orleans: 'Neither I nor others, when we were with her, had ever evil thoughts; there was in her something divine'.

Proofs of Joan's sanctity there are in abundance. 'All the soldiers regarded her as a saint' (Barbin, of Poitiers). We need not wonder that people kissed her feet and her hands when she passed on horseback. Her judges, of course, made this, too, an accusation. 'But they kissed my hands as little as I could manage,' was her pleasant answer. 'I leave all to God, my Creator; I love Him with all my heart.'

They wished to make her out bloodthirsty, and asked her which she preferred – her banner or her sword?

'More – forty times more – my banner than my sword!' And she said further: 'I have never killed anyone.'

With regard to this same banner, they asked her further: 'Which helped the other more, you or your standard?'

'Whether the victory was of my standard or of myself, it was all Our Lord's.'

'Was your hope of victory founded upon your standard or upon yourself?'

'It was founded upon Our Lord, and upon no other.'

'If another than you had carried that standard, would he have had as good fortune as you?'

'Of that I know nothing. I leave it to Our Lord.'

She is the image of heroic obedience; and what her obedience earned was the charge drawn up by the Canon d'Estivet, the detailed act of accusation wherein Joan was described as 'a witch, a sooth-sayer, a fortune-teller, a false prophetess, one who invoked evil spirits, superstitious, an adept in the magical arts, ignorant of the Catholic faith, schism-atic, suspect of breaches of the article of the Creed, *One*, *Holy Church*, and other articles, sacrilegious, idolater, apostate, evil in word and deed, a blasphemer of God and the saints, scandalous, seditious, a disturber of the peace, a promoter of war, cruelly athirst for human blood and the cause of its shedding, totally and shamelessly regardless of the decency and the conventions of her sex, having irreverently taken the garb and the state of a soldier. . . .'

But what aroused fiercest indignation was her obedience to 'God first served'. She replied wisely, and at first smilingly, because her voices had told her 'Have good courage and a cheerful face' – then, suffering too much, she grew weary and amazed to find what was in their minds. Whenever a question was of great gravity, she asked for a delay that she might take counsel of her voices. Her voices told her to reply 'boldly'. She replied boldly; so boldly that she exasperated her judges. Whenever possible she mentioned the name of the King of France, Charles VII, whose treachery she did not know and whom she was to love with all her might to the end, seeing in him the lieutenant of Jesus Christ. Never was she intimidated by the solemnity of a lie brought against her. They questioned her about St. Michael and her saints.

'I have told you what I know; but rather than tell you all I know I would have you cut off my head.'

She refused the oath again and again, for she

detested sacrilege. She would reply upon oath only to what concerned the trial: 'That is not in the charge. Spare me; pass on', was her constant phrase. She had certain jests, especially with regard to the English, which could not have been much to the taste of Maître Cauchon and his servile creatures. 'As to the English, the peace they need is to go home to England.'

Yet they put her in a difficulty when they made statements that she could not understand as to the difference between the Church triumphant, with which she was already in living contact, and the Church militant, wherein she could see none but enemies of the truth – enemies, that is, of Jesus Christ.

'Do you submit to the decision of the Church?' Her reply is profound and luminous in its psychology.

'I submit to God, Who sent me, to Our Lady and to all the saints of Paradise. *And it seems to me that it is all one – God and the Church –* and that one ought not to make so much difficulty about it. Why do *you* make it a difficulty?'

What she would not say upon any pretext was that she had not seen what she had seen, nor heard what she had heard. But they remained sublimely themselves. 'If such things have appeared to you, do not believe in them. The belief you have in such things, you must repel. Believe rather in the words and the opinions of the University of Paris. . . .'

Assuredly it was not by the Church Militant that Joan was condemned. It was the English who condemned her, using as their instrument a Bishop in their pay who was not really Archbishop of Rouen. Besides, Joan did make an act of good-will in regard to this ecclesiastical tribunal. It was at the time of her abjuration; her voices reproached her bitterly for it; yet it makes it impossible to say that she refused formal obedience to the Church militant. But in fact the Court was only a caricature of the Church and showed itself for a caricature when it rejected Joan's appeal to be heard in Rome. Ysambard de la Pierre gave evidence at the rehabilitation process in 1450 that he had himself copied out for the Bishop of Avranches this decision of St. Thomas:

'In doubtful matters concerning the faith, one must always have recourse to the Pope or a General Council.'

The Maid demanded that she be tried by the Pope 'whom, after God, she acknowledged'. As Rome was far away, Ysambard suggested to her that she should submit her case to the Council of Bâle, where were gathered men of the King of France's party. It was upon this point that Cauchon hurled at Ysambard his famous 'Shut up, in the Devil's name!' And the Maid's desire to submit herself to the General Council was calmly ignored.

At the beginning of her trial Joan had pleaded that there should be summoned to judge her 'ecclesiastics of the French party equal in number to the ecclesiastics of the English party'. They did

not bother to reply, any more than to her plea to
be kept in an ecclesiastical prison. Whenever the
Church would have been on her side, it would
appear that it was no business of the Church.

At the moment when no suffering was spared
her that man could inflict, God obtained from this
girl who had always 'served Him first', an evidence
of weakness – that sudden weakness which He uses
to bind to Himself still more closely the soul that
has known it. It was in appearance, and for the
moment it was in fact, a complete surrender on
Joan's part. She stood in the Place St. Ouen,
terrified of the flames, seeing nothing, lost to all
understanding; fearing that she had been deceived
by her voices, which had promised her deliverance
and had now abandoned her; not knowing whether
to laugh wildly, or to die in an agony of grief. She
was under the pressure of the urging of the worthy
Massieu, who did everything to save her; she was
crushed under the priestly accusations which, like
a rain from hell, beat upon her from the mouth of

a famous preacher. Unbearable, too, was the mysterious sentence formulated against the poor child by the Bishop of Beauvais. Before the reading of the sentence was finished, Joan cried out in a loud voice:

'I wish to hold all that the Church orders, and that you, judges, wish to say and pronounce; in all I submit to your orders'.

They made her repeat in a strangled voice some words read out by Massieu; then they gave her to sign as best she could[1] an abominable confession – a retraction on all points of what she had said before, a string of insults against herself, which was in no way what she had repeated after Massieu; for, remember, she could not read. At that moment her heart was in the depth of the abyss.

From that time Joan's distress was immeasurable, and the darkness grew deeper about her mind and her will. This detestable abjuration was the ultimate despoiling, the horrible dregs of the

[1] She signed with a little circle, and an Englishman took her hand and guided it, so that she wrote her whole name, followed by a cross.

58

chalice. They condemned her now, not to the flames, but to a perpetual imprisonment, 'with the bread of sorrow and the water of anguish that you may weep your faults, that you may not again commit what you will have to weep for henceforth'.

Joan returned to her prison, accepted the woman's clothing they gave her, took off those that Christ Our Lord had caused her to take, and, feeling that her heart was dead, she let them shave off her hair. . . .

Four days later – her voices having reproached her with having 'damned her soul to save her life' – and a lustful officer having tried to violate her by night – Joan resumed her soldier's garb. To her judges, who came to her prison where they found her sobbing heart-brokenly, she confessed that her abjuration was only pretence, and she proclaimed that she maintained for ever that which she had retracted. In any case she would rather die immediately than be in chains all her life. This was the

Monday. On the Wednesday, May 30, 1431, towards nine in the morning, she was led out on to the Place du Vieux Marché, near the Church of St. Sauveur. She wore woman's dress.

A multitude had gathered; ten thousand people to see her last agony. They made her mount the scaffold; then Nicolas Midi uttered the words precedent to excommunication:

'We declare you a decayed member; and that you may not corrupt others, rejected from the unity of the Church, separated from its body, abandoned to the secular power, we reject you. . . .'

At the moment of her leaving the prison, Joan had made her confession to Friar Martin Ladvenu. That was the moment of her 'Eloi, Eloi, lama sabacthani' – all had been torn from her. She no longer even knew what she must think of her voices, which had told her of a great victory and a deliverance at hand, and had promised that she 'would come finally to the Kingdom of Paradise'. All was dark.

At this last moment everything converged towards one point – the reality of human wickedness. In her memory she no longer distinguished the angel of Chinon from herself. It seemed to her now that it was no angel who brought the crown to the Dauphin, but only herself. Of the angels who thronged about her at Chinon, few were with her now – scarcely any. Her world was closing in: there was the Lord Jesus Christ and there was Joan, with her mission, about to be immolated, consumed by the fire, holy, unacceptable, superfluous, a decayed member.

'Maître Pierre, where shall I be this night?'

'Have you, then, no hope in God?'

'Yes, and with God's aid I shall be this night in His Kingdom of Paradise.'

She received Our Lord's Body with so much devotion, such shedding of tears, that no words could express it. So says her confessor. And from that instant she ceased not to pray. But when she remembered that she was to be burned, she began to lament terribly: 'Alas, must they treat me so horribly and so cruelly that my body, whole and entire, which was never corrupted, must to-day be consumed and brought to ashes! . . . I call God, the Great Judge, to witness the great wrong that is done to me!'

Many theologians were troubled in mind, and withdrew. The few friends whom Joan's sweetness had won, remained with her. All the world wept: the judges, the crowd of Burgundians, the very English. The face of the infamous Loyseleur who had acted the traitor in her regard was bathed in tears; each man, no doubt, looking upon the wicked spectacle, thought pityingly of his own kindness. When she had heard the sermon through and knew the sentence which delivered her, as one relapsed, to the secular arm, Joan remained a half hour in that sublimest prayer, wherein she asked pardon of God, and gave pardon to men. She wanted to have a cross, and an Englishman made her a small cross with a piece of wood. She kissed it with devotion and put it in her breast. Further, she begged Massieu to bring the cross from the church that she might look upon it all the time she was dying. Having it, she kissed it passionately and kept hold of it until she was led to the stake. The English soldiers were tired of the whole business, and anxious to have done. They thrust Massieu violently away, and one of them hurled at him: 'What, priest, do you want us to dine here?' Then came the order: 'Do your duty!' They led Joan to the stake which was set on a slab of plaster. They bound her firmly to it. In the flames she ceased not for one moment to look upon the great cross from the church, which Friar Martin Ladvenu held before her as high as he could, that she might nail her own soul upon it. In that moment her will was totally one with the Will of her Lord, and she had no word but the Name of Jesus on her lips. 'Jesus! Jesus!' she cried out; then she spoke no more, and they thought that she was dead.

As her clothes had caught fire the English

'commanded the executioners to draw the flames aside an instant, that she might be seen by all the crowd'. Then the flaming wood was replaced.

Her body was not completely destroyed by the fire. The executioner 'in spite of the oil and sulphur and coal that he heaped thereon, could not succeed in burning the Maid's heart'. He saw in this a miracle and, in an excess of despair he cried aloud: 'We are all lost; we have burned a saint!'

This was likewise the judgment of the Church militant which, twenty-five years after, rehabilitated Joan, and, five centuries after, canonized her.

Ysambard de la Pierre made this deposition, of which it would be sinful to omit one word:

'An English soldier who hated her more than can be said, had sworn to bring a faggot to the pyre. He did so, and having at that moment heard Joan call upon the Name of Jesus, he remained stricken and, as it were, in ecstasy at the sight. His friends took him to a tavern close by the Vieux Marché and gave him to drink that he might

64

regain his strength. In the afternoon this same Englishman confessed in my presence to a Friar Preacher – an Englishman like himself – that he had been altogether wrong; that he had great regret for what he had done that morning; and that he no longer believed Joan guilty. He affirmed that, at the moment when she rendered up her soul, he had seen a white dove flying heavenward.'

IV

IN 1449, the English having capitulated as Joan had prophesied, Charles VII entered the town of Rouen with great pomp. He remained there rather more than a week with his mistress, Agnes Sorel. To one who comes from reading the documents on the death of Joan of Arc, there is something immeasurably painful in the description given by the chronicler of the magnificence of his entry, and of the festival that followed.

'*The King of France celebrated the Feast of All Saints at St. Catherine, near Rouen; then, on the Monday following, he set out to make his entry into the town, accompanied by great lords grandly and richly attired.*

'*First rode the Comte de Sainct-Pol, mounted on a charger caparisoned in black satin, threaded with gold. After him, his pages and their steeds attired in like material; then came the groom apparelled like the other pages, leading a great charger, all covered with cloth of gold to the feet. The Comte de Nevers had twelve gentlemen with him, their horses caparisoned in pink satin with great white crosses.*

'The King of France was mounted and fully armed, on a horse covered to the feet with blue velvet sewn with lilies embroidered in gold; on his head was a cap of red velvet, gold threaded; behind him his pages clad in red, their sleeves all broidered with gold, who carried his helmet covered with fine gold in divers sorts and ostrich feathers of divers colours.

'At his right was the King of Sicily; at his left the Comte de Maine, his brother, all in white, their horses richly caparisoned and covered with white crosses sewn with gold thread, and their pages likewise.

'The Sieur de Cullant came after on a courser richly apparelled; round his neck a scarf of fine gold hanging down to his horse's crupper, and before him his pages. He was in charge of a squadron of six

hundred lances. On each one a pennant of red satin with a golden sun. . . .

And so the magnificence rolls on through page after page of the chronicle. At the gate of the town, the King was met by the Archbishop with many bishops, abbots and great churchmen. Dunois presented the citizens, come to ask the King's pardon for having so long withheld submission.

'Command was given that all the bells of the town should ring and that all citizens should cease from all work for a week and should make festival upon the King's coming. And there were besides minstrels in great numbers playing in the streets and at the cross-roads where the King must pass, upon divers instruments. . . .

'And in the windows were ladies old and young in great abundance, and the wives of the burgesses, richly attired, among them the Comtesse de Dunois; with whom were brought Talbot and all the English

hostages.   The said Lord Talbot wore that day a long velvet robe trimmed with fur given him by the King, and was there till all the company had passed by. . . .'

It was eighteen years since Joan of Arc had been burnt on the Place du Vieux Marché. Delicately, Charles VII preferred not to reawaken so unpleasant a memory. There is a time for sowing; there is a time for enjoying the harvest. It was only after the death of his mistress the following year that the good Charles remembered that the poor girl had been burnt for him – unjustly perhaps – in this town of Rouen, where so warm a welcome had awaited him, where a certain Nicolas Midi had preached his welcome in a moving sermon.

Thinking of this, he got as far as wondering if it might not be a good idea to set on foot an inquiry into the whole matter, but he soon gave it up, the thing being too complicated and, in any case, rather expensive. He felt that he might safely leave to God the fate of that unhappy Maid who had *come from the Bois Chesnu and had ridden on the backs of archers*, who had made him such curious predictions, who had dragged him off to Reims.

The outline was beginning to fade of this youthful memory. What point was there in going back over it? The Maid was dead these twenty years; Charles was not God, only God's vassal; he could not bring her back to life.

The Church militant had now only to look for her in the starry heaven of the Church triumphant.